Robert Miltner

Horse Skull Moon

SV

SurVision Books

First published in 2024 by
SurVision Books
Dublin, Ireland
Reggio di Calabria, Italy
www.survisionmagazine.com

Cover image: the marble sculpture of a horse's head by Pheidias, from Parthenon, currently kept in the British Museum

Design © SurVision Books, 2024

ISBN: 978-1-912963-51-5

Acknowledgments

Grateful acknowledgment is made to the editors of the following, in which some of these poems, or versions of them, originally appeared.

Journals:

AMP Magazine: "Avenue of the Insurgents"
Cloudbank: "Hunting the Cutty Wren"
Concīs: "Soldier Child"
CutBank Literary Journal: "Flood Plain," "Fracture," and "Monochromatic Photograph"
Full Bleed: "Québec Express," "Stand of Snakes" and "What We Were"
JuxtaProse: "August Tilt"
Midwest Review: "School Closing"
Rubbertop Review: "Circle, Rectangle, Square, Box"
Slush Pile Magazine: "A Waking Sea" and "City of Salt"
Wildness Eco Folio: "Snow, Rust, Dust, Coal"

Anthologies:

Dreaming Awake: New Contemporary Prose Poetry from the United States, Australia, and the United Kingdom (MadHat Press, 2023): "Cicatrix Vortex," "Drifting Continents," and "Stranger in a Familiar Suit"

The epigram is from Federico Garcia Lorca's poem "Ruin".

"City of Salt" borrows its title from the novel by Abdelrahman Munif.

"Hunting the Cutty Wren" is a Celtic solstice song that evolved into an anarchist song during the 1381 British Peasant's Revolt.

CONTENTS

*it was clear that the moon
was a horse's skull,
and the air, a dark apple*

—Federico Garcia Lorca

Drifting Continents

You are living temporarily in concrete islands of the night, at the ramparts of sinking cities, somewhere outside the capital of sorrows   You are the all-mobile insomniac   Among remnants of radical division, you are chronically fracturing   You are the collapse of speculative futures discovered among archeologically recovered skulls of primates whose history is hieroglyphs cannibalistically scraped and recorded by canines, molars, and incisors You are a suicide note composed from unspoken vocabularies comprised of faltering metaphors, oxidizing hinges, broken crowbars, lost anchors You are a troubadour tell-tale of failing glaciers and disappearing peninsulas You are the fragmented song lyrics of our return to the sea

Avenue of the Insurgents

Chromium yellow used to be its own country   Borderless lands
traversed by nomads and geologists, cartographers and bandits
A stain near a dull green sea shows a tangerine incursion like a
root canal, a citrus cavity, blood orange spilled on lemon cloth
Paint as serration, secession, sedition   As dream of breaching
boundaries and coastlines   Territories tint and bleed beyond
map or frame or time or rhyme or tune   Before the incarnadine
ocean pooled, royal blue was a standing stone

Hermes Astride the Sea

Months without rain and gale force winds from the west like gas
jets   A wildfire racing over a mountain top is a runaway herd
of terrified horses   A torched small town explodes like a bomb
test   There is no place for the fiery surge to go except down
Orange, yellow, and red flames enact a frenzied dance below a
billowing dome of acrid smoke   Leaping the highway that
winds through the coastal valley, it lands, a rogue comet,
fractures into scornful flames sprinting toward the sea's
breaking waves   Burning fast across the water's surface, it is a
spectacle like a sunset, like a volcanic ignition   Like the rumored
edge of where the earth ends

Québec Express

Terrifying space trapped in a limited canvas   Dazzling snow
etching the horizon, disappearing into periphery's nearly
impervious border   An immense white scene is disrupted by
stands of conifers forging obsidian humps along a liminal
division   A smoke-colored sky clouds a coal-dust stratosphere
The arrival of graphite and steel lines divides the vanishing point
from its widening panorama, its curve slight as a migratory bird
trajectory: beak or eye or maw or pincer   A tremor of a rapid
mammal constructed of iron and rust   The past bearing down
to erase the future

Dancers on a Frozen Lake

Freezing drizzle laces Lake Erie   Sleet warps a graying sky
Beneath a glazing surface secrets sleep in shale strata   Snow
defines the coastline: drifts and eddies and swirls   Waves
frozen while cresting, capping   Along flat landscape shores
translucent forms shiver, stop   Scarecrows to statues to
dancers to paused kimonos   Kabuki figures poising to perform
from Buffalo to Cleveland to Toledo   Winter embroidery is ice
stitch is silver weft is silk crepe   The horizon line shivering,
leaning, locking   When Hermes arrives, the solid moment
shatters

A Waking Sea

The winter sky tears, a glacier falls, air pressures   Not twang of
bowstring   Not screech of tectonic plates   Not blow-up of
concrete towers   But heft and weight   But cleave and crevice
But vibration and explosion   Ice shelves moan   Coasts and
peninsulas submerge   Precipices cascade like reams of blank
pages, chronicle the drowning moment   Master Wind ablates
the ice, shelf to sheen to mirror to silver to pearl to frost to
white to breathless blue   As gravity leans on glaciers, they
crack and calve, slump and quake, collapse and plummet
Against the thin dome of polar sky, a cataclysm of glass slivers,
reverberates: aural thunder to tactile thrum

School Closing

You set the aperture for an establishing shot   Looming gray skies grow darker over a Rust Belt city, storm clouds spreading like smoke from chemical fires   The lens centers on the horizontal architecture of an abandoned red brick elementary school, the rising staircase, the double door entryway   Empty vertical rectangles of broken-out windows reduce their reflection to sparkling shards of glass   Dark-eyed Juncos fly through empty frames of space

You plan an historical montage   Sepia panorama shows scaffolding, brick-layers, hod-carriers, men wearing dull overalls and flat caps, their bandanas flapping good-bye from back pockets   A black and white long shot captures rows of students standing in hallways, thin lines of children clutching books and lunch bags as they file into a classroom   A close-up of the arms-folded teacher, tall as a traffic signal, establishes atmosphere, balance, tone

You close with a panoramic photograph   A corroded metal utility pole meant to carry electricity, a wooden telephone pole with its cross arms an obscure ideogram, all the lines fallen from disuse, disrepair, despair   Dusk, and chimney swifts circle a leaning schoolhouse smokestack   A swirling of feathers, wings, claws, and beaks drops like rocks   Bats arrive, swoop, unstitch and restitch ragged edges of the frantic night sky

13

City of Salt

Follow the burning inside your sinuses, nostrils, throat   Walk
the rue of lamentation that stings like bitter sugar   It is a city
constructed over evaporated estuaries by sailors, mariners,
seafarers, seadogs   You will know it by its three sodium pillars
The scent is like chloride from glazed fjords of the crystalline
north   You will know it by its brackish script written on paper
blotters dissolving in the lost arroyos   You will know it as a salt
flat with fault lines, as a black ice gleam in summer heat   Hear
the song of the pinch, the grain, the saline drop   You will know
it as a blanched map in your hands   As briny geography sifting
through your softened fingers: rock, road, marsh, sea

Snow, Rust, Dust, Coal

The woods of the Cuyahoga Valley wear silence like fresh
snowfall   Stands of oak trees could be abandoned houses
Frames of roofless homes show siding sliding from structure,
plaster falling from lath   Lintels and sills of doorframes remain
open   Wrens fly through glassless windows empty as eyes of
roadkill   It could be a Rust Belt city like Cleveland, Akron,
Youngstown, Toledo, Elyria, Sandusky   Or a coal mining town
where two roads cross in the Meigs County Appalachian foothills
Places where sad ballads of busted dreams are sung in minor
keys   Hope stays silent as mice in snow, frail to falter to fail to
stillness   Crows defeather the body, strip the skin   Ants
follow pheromone paths, scrape the skeleton   Leaves cover
what remains   Sleet to ice to freezing insistence shatter aged
bones   Summer scorches farms into autumn droughts
Displaced shadows settle into tinged soil: a cicatrix amidst the
text of the earth

Cicatrix Vortex

See the blind mime lost in a cave   Rocks imitate embedded anthracite, ambered insects, inverted coral, petrified bone Deception to dalliance to damage as aggressive cells encamp as newly discovered graves: tendril to kneecap to cheekbone to spine to curve of skull   Owls burrow to nest in abandoned wolf ledges, dry wells, sinkholes, any divot or culvert that won't hard scab   Low water draws toward duckweed ponds   Toward places white-brown cattails, yellow iris, black willow push down scaly roots   Where solitary moles move slowly under moonless nights   Where trails of passed fox appear as scuffed stones or scraped surface between toad trillium or spiderwort   Where black bat moths spread menacing wings   Where the chrysalis cracks

Fracture

Sunlight blazes over a canvas of Western plains   Rectangular farmsteads, linen-thread county roads, rolling contours formed by glaciers and insistent shallow river beds   Flowing through tubular canals from northern tar sands to coastal shipping ports, a pipeline is a running fence that crosses fiercely over border shadows, aquafers, subterranean watercourses, sacred lands Movement of the opium dram of corvine ink is incursive, insistent, voracious

Dogs bark a graphite melancholy   Coyotes howl malignant as rust-jawed necromancers   Crows displace a red-tail hawk, finish what it had caught   Body and skin are flayed, ruptured, cleft from bone to marrow to maw to broken bellows of jaw

The spill reveals its seditious secrets as blood tints soil: an immiscible ointment imping sacrifice to slick gods   Geography leans in on itself, heft to depth to density to balance   The inversion is an unannounced eclipse of ravens, a collapsed tornado, a swindling sea of rising crude, a pristine prairie displaced by a black hole

The Tunnel

Train windows frame the moving slideshow, a stereoscope,
fanned sets of postcards   Tracks follow the Mediterranean Sea
south from Miglio to Genova   Rows of cream and rose-colored
three story apartment buildings   Laundry drying on balconies
Small single block cemeteries   Open space of corner parks
Stone houses surrounded by orchards of fig trees, trellises of
yellow, orange, red Bougainvillea over doorways

A shallow river rock-jumbled and crossed over by an arched
steel bridge   Failing or abandoned warehouses soot-grayed by
time, roofs caving like broken-into crypts   Skeletal metal-
framed greenhouse with spidered glass catching, splaying
sunlight   Bell towers and church spires, adorned by figures of
patriarchs, saints, ghosts pointing to an emptying sky

Azure to indigo into black as the train plunges into a tunnel local
workers blasted and hewed for years through hard mountain
stone   It's the line connecting with the shadowed labyrinthian
alleyways of Old Genova   It's a brisk visit to the catacombs, the
afterlife, the inferno, to Hades, to the underworld   A Metro
going nowhere   It's the sudden subway to the capital of
sorrows

August Tilt

Hermes as barometer of displacement and migration   He impersonates cairns of stone waiting in middles of deserts or atop arid mesas   Imps the uniformed guards at urban checkpoints, his clipboard and sidearm appropriate props for an impostor   Inside his satchel: a stolen salver, four silver coins stamped with a rooster on one side, a goat on the other   It's all just surface work, exercises in the prose of survival

Hermes as an orphan child seeking the unmarked borders of the night   As a thousand flicked lighters shaping new constellations In brokerage between the visible and the unseen, transition is trouble is trial is trauma   Rights-of-way lined with cyclone fences, textured eyes to mouths to fists, the images of unwelcoming cities   A packed deportation train departs, disappears in the direction of the regime of uncertain fears

Hermes as elegiac art funneling ashes of children bombed into the eye socket of the earth   The gaseous mouth of the afterlife, the hole where snakes slither, disappear   So the turn of his wrist is release of a match, the small flame falling like a suicide from a bridge, the splendor of ignition, the wall of wildfire racing down into the parched canyon, the fires burning across the skin of the river and racing toward the refugee camp on the other side of the closed bridge

Hunting the Cutty Wren

O where are you going? says Public to Private   You should not disclose that, says Lawyer to Lie   We're off to the city, with sad Mistress Pity, where quarried stone walls do padlock so princely

What will you do there? says Irate to Pirate   Speak to my counsel, says Grifter to Graft   We'll take down their trees, says Reader to Raider, to batter and breach stout oaken gates, says Philly the Tweet

Who'll pay us to do this? says Congress to Wrongness   And not blame us to witness? says Lacky to Luck   No coins in my pocket, says Cyclops the drunk   No keys in my cowl, claims False Friar, a bald-pated monk

Who'll cut up this cutty? says Murder to Mortar   No wren hen, not I, says Pester to Fester   How butcher the body? says Cleaver to Clever   Dull saws and fish knives and jawbones of primates, says bold and bare-footed Master Jax the Axe

How should we cook cutty? says Randy the Red Nose   Up with the kettle and down with the pan, says Andy the Brown Nose, as fast as we can   Make supper of loam and cold river stone, uneaten by children border-crossing drowned, says Nate of the Gate to Jack of the Land

What manner for eating said dead wren? says Bone to China   With butter knives and fingers, soup spoons and sporks, basters and tongs, says Hobnob to Robin   And pick between our teeth with cutty's pulled feathers, says Pitchfork to Dirk

And who gets the tongue? says Prefect to Pervert   And who
the spleen? says Venom to Snake   And who the blood? says
Cutter to Stab   We need not tell you, says Older to Moulder

And who gets the Cutty wren's bloody red heart? says Lover to
Other   O the poorest and weakest, the drained and the fallow,
says sad Mistress Pity to Scavenger Sparrow

Soldier Child

Two dark oak doors with white porcelain knobs frame a boy of
thirteen   He wears an unbuttoned double-breasted coat
clutched at his chest by his left hand   A turned-up collar
Cropped hair dark as hardwood floors   Bare feet and jeans
with torn knees   White bandage wound around his left ankle
The weight he won't put on it   The way he gazes back at you
His eyes black as the holes of gun barrels   The way he doesn't
blink

Monochromatic Photograph

A string snaps as Master Wind marionettes kite's frantic dance
Released from the cupped hands of a gust, kite tips and
trembles and plummets like a small airplane faltering from an
electrical stroke   Earth's magnetic pull grasps falling kite,
pushes it into the vast ocean of a failing farm field

Airplane is sparrow struck by escaped kite, is sparrow bleached
by sun glare to absence of color   White feathers scatter like
exclamation points beside the crashed crushed kite frame of
small bird

Three crows coast, land   They eat from the bowl of sparrow's
belly: ribs, sinew, muscle, intestines, until only empty cavity
remains   The corvid trio departs

Gathering clouds rumble and rift   White bird cup with
feathered tail fills with rain   Soon the scrap dealer buzzards
arrive, scavenge emptied hollow of sparrow kite plane   Master
Wind deranges the wreckage: a sky broken by lightning, a coup,
a species extinction

Circle, Rectangle, Square, Box

The frame; the mat; the linoleum into which the print is cut   An orchard row; an acre of corn; the vineyard and cellar   The block called home; the sandbox the cat sat in; a jack-in-the-box with a broken top   Sidewalk slate tilted by tree roots; the trap door in the stage floor; the card table the ghosts and aces came over   The room where the betrayal occurred; the garage door still open after the corpse was removed; a window framing a skull-white moon

Stranger in a Familiar Suit

Hermes arrives in your small town of sheep-white homes   Aged
sycamores cast dappled shade on the cobbled streets   The
nails of his boot heels rock for blocks   He barters in balms and
sweets with lonely wives and nervous girlfriends   The twin
scents of sin and salvation linger and languor under the gauze of
purity   You won't find him in that faded gray house across the
tracks   Or in the back of a rusted van parked down the dead
end alley   His brothers are shadows and chimney swifts   His
father a moonless night

Flood Plain

Seen from an airplane it's an erasure of edges   A river channel crested, breached   Mixture of drowned cornfields and layers of dark topsoil pressed from paint tubes   A chaotic convergence expressing vulnerability   Thick brown mudslide swaths applied with scrapers   Swirling slurry of coal waste leaked from earthen lagoons   Floating islands of docks, unmoored barns, warehouses   Oil leaking from ruptured refinery tanks   As snapped power lines ignite, red ribbons of fire incinerate shore's trees, shrubs, cattail marshes   Bridges closed, collapsing, submerging   Cut sections of gray linear highways resemble discarded sheet metal   A mangle of triangles, rectangles   A drowning of squares, circles   Silver flashes of sunlight on sudden-wrought water meadows, estuaries   Weather drones display deranged collages as fixed cartographies become action paintings

Stand of Snakes

Skeins of sheep-shorn wool asleep in a bowl   Woven snakes of
sundry colors coil   Twilling of thread waits in a flax ark
Basket of unwound and whorled line   Coat that envelops a
round of rope, of spooled python impatient to unsling   Fissures
split as yarn strands breach and spill like entrails   Tendrils
furrow and sleave   What was once twined splinters into
filament   Awakened from frozen ages of hibernation, hybrid
virus and helix of protoplasm germinate and cycle   Force from
inside walls pushes out, seeks pressure points where plaster
shatters   Sheet rock slates, faults, fractures: a mobile
disassembling   Except for wet pressed board, cheap plywood,
or warped knotty pine, what else is there to define structure?

Documentary Soundtrack

Steel bridges stand constructed above the winding Cuyahoga River mouth where wooden ferries once crossed   Old River lift rail bridge   Detroit-Superior arch bridge   Hope Memorial Lorain-Carnegie truss bridge   Peregrine falcons fly among a quartet of sandstone art deco pylons of Hermes wearing a winged helmet or laurel crown   Sirens, car horns, truck brakes The elemental music of aging architecture oxidizing   Fall storms shake structures until a taut, tonal resonance hums like mouth harps played by old gods   Like blues guitars, their stainless steel slides hovering over frets, the arc of their sound waves making the moment vibrate

Book of Ghosts

Recto page with dried plant specimen: stalk, root, fruit, flower, leaf   appended in place with aged tape   Affixed label written in a dead language   Verso page holds stained outline impression: a twin, a petrified handprint of an early human Object to memory to loss to shadow   Removed page held up to window light transforms into thinnest membrane: a portal, a pin-holed parchment-thin sheet through which to view the passing world   Hard sunlight erases images, brittles the paper: page to scrap to tear to relic

What We Were

A speck seen from space   One square black block   Shadows hiding beyond light   The silvered sky: airplanes and sky-scraping architecture   Jet lines as incisions into a blue tableau, a morning mural slashed by a fanatic attacker   Homes embossed on laid linen or graph paper or wasp nests   Ants burned crisp by ozone and methane drought   Steel reinforced concrete cracking, coiling, collapsing   Gravity thrashing like torn tendons amidst sounds of steel bridge supports snapping   Jack-knifed truck trailers as pop-up checkpoints   Coral reefs formed from rusted bottle caps   Sun-blistered sculptures built from bent snips of tin

Selected Poetry Titles Published by SurVision Books

Contemporary Tangential Surrealist Poetry: An Anthology
Edited by Tony Kitt
ISBN 978-1-912963-44-7

Invasion: An Anthology of Ukrainian Poetry about the War
Edited by Tony Kitt
ISBN 978-1-912963-32-4

Noelle Kocot. *Humanity*
(New Poetics: USA)
ISBN 978-1-9995903-0-7

Marc Vincenz. *Einstein Fledermaus*
(New Poetics: USA)
ISBN 978-1-912963-20-1

Helen Ivory. *Maps of the Abandoned City*
(New Poetics: England)
ISBN 978-1-912963-04-1

Tony Kitt. *The Magic Phlute*
(New Poetics: Ireland)
ISBN 978-1-912963-08-9

Clayre Benzadón. *Liminal Zenith*
(New Poetics: USA)
ISBN 978-1-912963-11-9

Thomas Townsley. *Tangent of Ardency*
(New Poetics: USA)
ISBN 978-1-912963-15-7

Mikko Harvey & Jake Bauer. *Idaho Falls*
  (Winner of James Tate Poetry Prize 2018)
  ISBN 978-1-912963-02-7

John Bradley. *Spontaneous Mummification*
  (Winner of James Tate Poetry Prize 2019)
  ISBN 978-1-912963-13-3

Charles Kell. *Pierre Mask*
  (Winner of James Tate Poetry Prize 2019)
  ISBN 978-1-912963-19-5

Charles Borkhuis. *Spontaneous Combustion*
  (Winner of James Tate Poetry Prize 2021)
  ISBN 978-1-912963-30-0

Noah Falck and Matt McBride. *Prerecorded Weather*
  (Winner of James Tate Poetry Prize 2022)
  ISBN 978-1-912963-39-3

Michael Zeferino Spring. *Kahlo's Window*
  (Winner of James Tate Poetry Prize 2022)
  ISBN 978-1-912963-40-9

Jeffrey Cyphers Wright. *Fuel for Love*
  (Winner of James Tate Poetry Prize 2023)
  ISBN 978-1-912963-45-4

George Kalamaras. *That Moment of Wept*
  ISBN 978-1-9995903-7-6

George Kalamaras. *Through the Silk-Heavy Rains*
  ISBN 978-1-912963-28-7

Order our books from http://survisionmagazine.com